the flap pamphlet series

Breaking the Surface

open, read, turn

Breaking the Surface

the flap pamphlet series (No. 15)
Printed and Bound in the United Kingdom

Published by the flap series, 2017
the pamphlet series of flipped eye publishing
All Rights Reserved

Cover Design by Petraski
Series Design © flipped eye publishing, 2010
Author Photo © Supal Desai, 2017

ISBN-13: 978-1-905233-50-2
Editorial work for this series is supported by the Arts Council of England

Breaking the Surface

Katie Hale

Contents | *Breaking the Surface*

i / The Find

(   )..9
The Find...11
The Raven Speaks 12
Let Me Tell You about the Wolf 14
How to Kill a Mermaid 16
Siren's Song..17

ii / Remains

Rain, Steam and Speed – The Great Western
    Railway 21
Wishes..22
Portrait of Depression as a Branch-Line Station....................24
Herculaneum 25
  – I – Erc46: The Bella Donna.....................25
  – II – Erc86: A Paterfamilias......................26
  – III – Erc49: A Labourer with Multiple Fractures..........27
  – IV – Erc132: An Upper-Class Child 28
  – V – Remains 29
Go into the Woods 30
In Memoriam 31

iii / Pearls

How the Sea Fought Back 35
Procedure 37
Secret..38
Gogyoshi for Jenny 39
The Cheese Mites (1903).................................40
You're in My Blood like Holy Wine..............41
Crockery 44
Eat Your Heart Out 45

----- I
The Find

(   )

after John McCullough

Apologetic, half-said,
you are two curved lips
forming words that will be read
as unnecessary, skimmed over
like a pebble is skimmed across a tide
or a fly is skimmed from a pot of water,
as though speaking out loud were something
to bend away from.

A corridor running the length
of a quiet house, you are made
only for connecting, a place
to be passed through and forgotten
the way a lover is let slip from the mind.

Let me worship you
in all your understated glory.
Let me unwrap
the dark mystery of your words,
balance them on the tip of my own tongue
till I understand your language,
the shapes of your voice
and how you encircle all of me.

You are hands cupped
(around sacred spring-water.)

You are diamond shell
(embracing an oyster.)

You are petals, folded
(over the protected treasure of a bee.)

The Find

We found a baby on the beach,
heard it crying first from the top
of the hill, its bagpipe lungs
turning the haar

to slanted music. We followed the sound
like gulls, to where it had scribbled
its body into a dip of sand;
its fists batted at waves,

fighting to push back
the maternal clutch of the water.
Its bald skin was red as the dawn,
cold, as though already part ocean.

We bundled it into our arms, fed it
on milk and the soft white of fish,
watched it grow. One night,
when the moon was full

and called all the weird
creatures of the deep
to surface, we heard
flapping from the cot:

switched on the light
to the slithering smell of fish,
a saltwater trail
towards the beach.

The Raven Speaks

'All the animals, birds, and fish will live in fear of you. They are all placed under your power.'
– Genesis 9:2

For a month or more, he kept us
in the dark, locked
in his mad tessellation of wood.

Through a slip of it, we could see
the lift and slump of horizon,
and on rougher days
shards of air forced themselves
through the gap.

When he took me
from the hull, led me up
and out towards the day...

to feel the chorus of sunlight on my feathers,
the freshness of salt
scouring from me the greyness of captivity...
when they unhooked my claw
from the metal ring, and made me soar –
is it any wonder I didn't come back?

I found land: a rocky
dump of mud and drowned fish,
the single resilient
olive branch. It stank
fierce as the ship I'd left behind.

I saw her coming,
that lily-winged dove. Hid.
Watched her pinch that little spurt of green
in her petite, pampered beak,
and promptly nip it, dead.

Let Me Tell You about the Wolf

Let me tell you about the wolf:
how he howled, how
his coal eyes
glittered, how his gait
was a leaf testing
the snow and with every muscled flex
he rippled. Around him, the air
sang, off-key and starving. He
was a spectrum of colour, a craving, his fur
like a hand on my skin, his predatory
circling. He stood on hind legs as though
he were a man, and I
knelt before him like a dog. At the rake
of claws across my back, I keened
like scratched alabaster,
begged him for
more.

Count to ten, he said,
and I did.

His breath was carnivore
hot on my stomach, my breasts,
my throat. My skin became
a thousand tiny flares,
became fur. I offered my blood
to his teeth, their yellow gleam
against vulnerable gums,

the stench of kills sighing
from his maw, and drained
myself to let him in…

But wolves are fickle. And wolves cannot be tamed.

I want to tell you
that I ripped his pelt
from his bones, wrapped it round
my body like a scent.

Or I want to tell you that
I left, found someone better,
a woodcutter
perhaps, a happy ever after.

Or I want to tell you that
when the tide is up, I prowl
along the shore, listen
to a distant wailing at the moon.

Instead, let me confess
how I led him
into the winter night, desiring
petals of blood in the snow, his dark
form shifting like a bruise, the ice
splintering – how there
he bent his body like a moan,
clasped me to him, committed
the worst betrayal a wolf can:
transformed
into a man.

How to Kill a Mermaid

Split her tail.
                    Take her fins and pull.
(There is no blood, but the smell
of rotting fish, and saltwater stinging
in the wound.)

                    Drop her on land
and make her dance, shedding scales
and stumbling, undressing her skin:
raw, and pink, and shining like a burn.

Hear her wailing like a curlew,
fingers wrinkled into fists against her eyes,
and tie her wrists

                    (it will not hurt) –

then push the girl away. Watch her

hobble home towards the sea
                    and drown.

Siren's Song

They came out of the mist: the old,
the young, the in-between,
knuckles big from rowing, palms
ringing from the brine. I'd seen

it all before. Even their faces
looked the same: their cheeks
sagging; foreheads dank with sweat;
eyes rattled by the squeak

of oars on rowlocks. Some were grey
with too much work and lack
of sleep. Some were burnt or blistered.
Some, when they pulled back

against the drift, made little moans
that made me think of men
dying on battlefields, till, on bending
forward, they cried again.

We couldn't help ourselves but sing.
To see men's faces lift,
hope rekindled in their eyes –
who wouldn't give the gift

of music? We poured out our notes
and hearts, became a balm
to lighten them, until they leapt
into the ocean's arms

to swim. The younger men laughed
and splashed each other. The old
murmured strange harmonies and talked
of home, till they shone cold

in the sunset. Their strokes weakened.
We held them, one by one,
as their hearts slowed. Our tune grew soft
and sad. Then they were gone.

----- ii
Remains

Rain, Steam and Speed – The Great Western Railway
after Turner

So slight it could almost be an accident
in the turmoil of colour and oil, racing
across the wingspan of the bridge
into the present – a flick of a hare

boxing the future, jacking its sharp angles
over dabbled green, its ears slipstreamed
to the focal point, and back legs springing
like a voice reaching the end of a question.

It runs to show man the limits of his progress.
It runs in terror of the industrial age.
It runs to demonstrate the engine's speed.
It runs because it is a hare and hares run.

Wishes

after Cairo Love Songs, *c. 1200 BC*

*

To be the signet ring
guarding her finger.

*

To be the copper face
that gazes all morning
from her mirror.

*

To push my hands through her hair
like the flowers she picks
on the river bank, where blue shoots
are lapis lazuli trapping the sun.

*

To wreathe my body
in her cast-off dresses
and the lingering warmth
of her limbs; to soak
her scarves till the fine weave
releases her scent.

*

To be her slave-girl
in summer; to bring her
wine, and dishes of berries
dark and fat with juice…

Portrait of Depression as a Branch-Line Station

A crippled platform, grass
eking through tarmac, signs
too weather-burnt to read,
the train, which they told me
I should get on, heaving off
with a sound like an old man
getting up from an armchair,
lumbering away along the line,
leaving only the wind, the hollow
howling wind, an empty track
I don't know how to walk down.

Herculaneum

I – Erc46: The Bella Donna

They say it ended with the ash:
searing the flesh from your skull
to leave only the delicate bridge
of your nose, a symmetrical jaw,
the twin pools of your orbits,
and the marble whiteness of teeth.

The way I picture it, you had a mouth
loud enough to crack the air, and a mind
sharper than splintered glass. I'd give you
a nose for a bargain, or an eye
to catch the eye of the man next door,
so beautiful you'd stop him in his tracks.

II – Erc86: A Paterfamilias

'Jogging... is itself
a form of prayer for an unknown future'
— Jacob Sam-La Rose, 'Rapture'

First, the swing: the metal disc balancing
on your fingertips as you mapped its arc
through the air, bearing its weight down
the muscled length of your arm. You spun,
propelling the disc higher and swifter until
you released, and watched it soar. Sometimes,
perhaps, you wondered how it would feel
to fly: without weight or expectation
or the heavy lag of wine. And sometimes,
when you ran, and felt your muscles stretch
and grow stronger, and felt the dust
quiver with your tread, you imagined
you could unhinge yourself from the earth
so quickly, you could outrun just about anything.

III – Erc49: A Labourer with Multiple Fractures

And sometimes, when your bones weighed
chill along the old breaks
and the smell of the horses lulled
you to sleep, then came the dream
of your brother singing:
the pipes and stops of his voice
keen and brief as a sparrow's.

IV – Erc132: An Upper-Class Child

And perhaps when you played on the beach,
you loved how the sun scattered lights
on the bay, how they shone like the ring
you weren't meant to wear in case you lost it –

the one you traded, five minutes per hold,
for a doll, a bowlful of dates, or honey
you ate from the jar, rubbing
the rough sugar over your teeth.

But the beads were your favourite prize:
bright glass, smooth as the stones
you skimmed over the waves, and when
you shook them, they rattled like leaves.
You rolled them between sticky hands
till they grew hot as the sun-beaten sand.

, upper-class child, spinning woman, flautist,
young shepherd, limping Maltese, man with
cutter, young fisher, old sailor, porter, javelin
, hunchback, old tailor, swimmer, shepherd with
slave girl, labourer with multiple fractures, bella
ged man, student, pregnant girl, banker, fat architect,
eather briefcase, coffin-bearer, piano teacher, high court
tist, newsreader, politician with wedding ring, one-
long-distance runner, actor with broken arm, computer
girl with two fillings, saxophonist, blind woman, tourist
era and spare batteries, boy with secondary bone cancer, pilot,
nuclear weapons tester, old man, woman, crouching child

Go into the Woods

Sling your knapsack across your back,
or spotted handkerchief over your shoulder.
The trees are close and thick in there –
do not hack the branches, or knock
the sick leaves down. Do not take a torch
or breadcrumbs. Let nobody follow you.
You can tell your story when you emerge.

If you emerge, you will not want
to tell your story. So
you will learn the look on disappointed faces.
Or, to pacify, tell how you once
witnessed
an owl, drift
in the mind of the trees, passing
wide as paper against the sky.

In Memoriam
i.m. P. N.

I can't say
what went through her head

as she dropped her bag and her book
and stepped over the edge of the platform

*

It's taken me four years to write this poem

----- iii
Shucking Oysters for Pearls

How the Sea Fought Back

A tale of the Gimuy Walubara Yidinji People

He tells a story old as the shore:
>a hunter in a wooden boat,
>the sixpence glitter of a fish,

>>the hunter's arm stretched, a swan's neck
>>before attack, elastic –

bolt of spear through flesh,
>>>red rust blood of the sea
>>turning the water to storm.

But this was not a catch
for supper, but a sacred fish,
a forbidden ray –

he tells how the ray
raised her wings, became
>albatross whirling
>>wind smack
>>>bird flap
>>>>book page flutter
>>>>>white underside
>>>>>catching the sun then hurling it back,
>>>>>the sea a furious
>>>>>broiling.

But that was fourteen thousand years ago.

Who now would taunt the rabid anger of the waves?
Who now would spear the sacred fish?

He fixes on the bitter past,
draws down his story of brine
        biting at the soles of his people

the long migration   inland.

Procedure

Lily. Daisy. Violet. Rose.

The routine dissection of flowers
is conducted on clinic-white benches,
in hidden back rooms, or on kitchen tables.

The setting is not important.
What matters is the delicate ministrations
of pollen-stained hands.

Specimen secured, the young stem
trapped and quivering, they raze
the nub from the top of the carpel.

Next, the petals, sheared
at the base and laid aside to shrivel
and turn black, the calyx wet to the air.

Last, the two leaves,
steepled so they meet like fingers
in prayer, then stitched –

a rough hatching of cotton
sewn flat, clean,
covering the screams of girls.

Secret

Against all odds, we keep her
locked in the dark space under the house.
It's a joint effort.
You bind her hands in complex knots
(it has been suggested she has the ability to pick locks),
chain one ankle to the ground.
I cover her with a blanket
to muffle her tinny, mewling sounds.
We feed her as seldom as possible.
We stop inviting the neighbours round,
change all our privacy settings to invisible.
We cut the phone line, lock the door,
nail the floorboards over our mouths.

Gogyoshi for Jenny

Tonight I holed the toe of your tights –
the ones from M&S I'd taken
to wearing: fitting my foot into the glove
of your foot, wrapping my legs in yours
like we were still a pair.

The Cheese Mites (1903)

For forty-nine seconds, their bodies
bump like the first blind life
or clockwork mice, fighting, a jerk and jolt
across the screen, cog-tooth legs
interlocking – so small
that for them the air is thicker
than water, they as deep as nightmare fish
heaving in the dark
of broken ships and whale bones,
where feelers twitch for sediment
to gorge and decompose:
it all comes down to this.

You're in My Blood like Holy Wine

The nights we came home drunk and every night,
we sat side by side, toes curled over the cliff
of the bed in your Oxford bedsit, and talked

about nothing. I know this, because it struck me
how precisely we controlled our breath,
how intricate each flex and shiver of skin

for words that no one cared about. We talked
about next door, the radio constant
through the brickwork, clutching at stations

before moving on. Sometimes, our arms
brushed and for a second, I spiralled
like smoke. There were always cigarettes

and the faint smell of apples, your burgundy
sweater, and the bristled curve of your throat.
There were dark thumbprints in the bowls

of old wine glasses, stacks of plates
like unopened letters, crumbs
sharp as insects littering the rug –

and all the words I didn't know how to say
were crows, flapping their frantic wings
against the inside of my mouth.

I swallowed, and they clawed my stomach
raw and sick. I've tried to drown them
in spirits, thick and toxic as the dark,

drown them till they tasted of nothing
but iron and burnt toast, and my body
was a smudge of wings on a pebble beach.

I've tried to speak. Once, I twisted my fingers
in the duvet, as if there would be ripples
that could reach you: your solid, immovable legs.

You shut the blinds, switched on the desk lamp
and Joni Mitchell – how *I could drink a case of you*
and I would still be on my feet – but before the end

you cut the track to watch the trailer
for the new James Bond. You said, *I know*
how you feel about me, and I believed you.

*

Remember the Church of the Assumption
of Our Lady in Mosta? Where the bomb
that plummeted through the roof in 1942

into the middle of a morning mass
without exploding was still on display,
and the little card proclaimed this a miracle

in several languages. Remember
how we watched it for almost twenty minutes,
how its silence filled the room

till we imagined we could hear it ticking:
a gunmetal heart; the weight of a hammer
raised above a head or bell

about to be struck; the stretched skin
of a drum anticipating thunder?
Or maybe it was just our own blood

beating against our ears like fists
against a door. Remember how I said, *I wish
it would do something drastic, I wish it would explode?*

Crockery

hard white seeds that don't grow in the ground

The word has left you. Instead, you turn
your plate-like hands, the way a ploughshare
turns up rocks, or the bones of small mammals.
You stare at the creases in the loose squares
of your palms, as though each
is a path you've never travelled.

Sometimes, we try to follow them –
trace them back down all the years
to when their route was still uncut: farm tracks
not yet tarmacked, or sheep trods across
a common field, where footsteps still raised
a breath of dry earth; where the seeds,
secreted in the ground, would wake in later months
as beetroot, potatoes, carrots, parsnips, swede.

Eat Your Heart Out

Once you've scythed the breast's white silk
and gnawed through the brittle sternum;
once you've unlocked the ribcage
as though slotting your bottom teeth
between two halves of an oyster;
once you've pressed your mouth between
the spongy lungs, rent the delicate veins,
and ripped capillaries with your tongue –

then you come to the heart, in its coat
of gleaming fat, still beating, a balled fist
pulsing as surely as sonar: if anything
carries the spark of life, it's this.

The blood soon cools in your throat.
It tastes of iron, sharp as ancient seas.

Acknowledgements

The Find was commended in the Ware Poetry Competition 2015;
The Raven Speaks was commended in the York Literature Festival /
YorkMix Poetry Competition 2016; *Let Me Tell You about the Wolf*
first appeared in issue 57 of The North; *How to Kill a Mermaid* was
originally published as part of online collection Poems Underwater;
Siren's Song first appeared in anthology *Lines Underwater; Rain, Steam
and Speed – The Great Western Railway* was shortlisted for the Wirral
Festival of Firsts Poetry Competition 2013, and was published on
The Compass; *Go into the Woods* and *The Cheese Mites (1903)* were
first published in Cadaverine Magazine; *Secret* first appeared in
Volume 102:4 of Poetry Review; *You're in My Blood like Holy Wine*
was shortlisted for the Ballymaloe International Poetry Prize 2016;
Crockery and *Eat Your Heart Out* were first published in *Mill* anthology
(Templar Poetry) in 2015.

Wishes is a versioning of sequences of Cairo Love Poems found in
translation in: *The Song of Songs and the Ancient Egyptian Love Songs*, by
Michael V. Fox; and *Love Lyrics of Ancient Egypt*, translated by Barbara
Hughes Fowler. *Herculaneum* is inspired by: *Herculaneum: Past and
Future*, by Andrew Walllace-Hadrill; and 'Health and Nutrition at
Herculaneum: An Examination of Human Skeletal Remains', by Sara
Bisel and Jane Bisel, in *The Natural History of Pompeii*, ed. Wilhelmina
Feemster Jashemski & Frederick G. Meyer.

I am grateful for support from the Wordsworth Trust, the University
of St Andrews, and Barbican Young Poets, and for Kim Moore's
workshops, where ( ), *The Raven Speaks*, and *Portrait of Depression as a
Branch-Line Station* were created.